Why Tennis

Tennis Tips For Young Competitors and Their Parents

GF Denehy

ISBN-13:978-0692406762
ISBN-10:069240676X

DEDICATION

To all the youth out there who haven't discovered just how
wonderful tennis can be - come and join us!

CONTENTS

ACKNOWLEDGMENTS

There are so many people in my tennis life that have taught me so much about the real benefits of tennis that I could not possibly mention them all. But, I have to acknowledge the one person without whom I could not have achieved so much in my tennis life—she put up with all my complaining about aches and pains, forgave my spending so much time and money on this one sport and stayed with me, even though I know she thought about putting my racquet somewhere close to my head, but didn't, my wife, Mamie.

.

1 TENNIS

It's early Sunday morning in January, it's 9 degrees outside with near blizzard conditions, the roads are icy and snow packed, I have a forty-five minute drive in front of me and I am not on my way to work or even going out into this mess to fix a downed power line. I am on my way to play tennis.

What's not to love about tennis!

TENNIS—it's such an easy game, all you have to do is hit the ball over the net! ...right!

The public perception about tennis is that it only takes place at expensive country clubs for rich people. New players often feel out of place and awkward since they don't even know how to keep score or how a tennis match is conducted or what you have to do to win. The new player generally has had no directions about how to become good, or even just what good is.

A new player will usually try the local park and recreation programs which will only provide them with the ability to hit the ball over the net. However, at the park and recreation the player may find out about all types of leagues, clinics, tournaments and tennis clubs. In further exploring this sport, the new player encounters private lessons, court fees and tournament fees. The realization begins to dawn that there is more to tennis than running down to the park to get in a quick game, and still no one has explained how to choose a racquet, which balls to use, what type of shoes to use, how to find the right people to play and practice with, how long it takes to get good enough to play in local tournaments, what to do to get good enough to win, the NTRP ranking system or even what the proper court etiquette is while on the tennis court, let alone what to wear.

So why would anyone, child or adult, want to continue to learn the game of tennis?

2 THE GAME

I have a tennis buddy named Jerry. By his win/loss record, he is one of the top players in most of the state of Ohio. He plays in multiple tournaments (big and small) throughout the year and wins most of them. He is nationally ranked and is really a nice guy.

Jerry and I will face off in tournaments three or four times a year. Jerry doesn't have any overpowering shots but his shot placement is remarkable. We always split sets and he always wins in the third. Jerry's game is very controlled and consistent. My game is what most people call a "big" game. I hit and serve hard. I get a lot of aces and a lot of ground stroke winners, but I am inconsistent. I win most of my matches, but not as many as Jerry.

If I want to beat Jerry, I have to either change my game or become more consistent. The problem is I like my game. I like hitting "big" ground stroke winners and I like serving aces. So, I have decided to become more consistent through more practice and more playing (which gets me on the court more often). I don't have to change my game to gain respect from my peers and I am not going on the pro circuit any time soon. Beating Jerry is not the focal point of my tennis. Tennis is not about just winning, it is about having fun on the court and enjoying the competition, the camaraderie, the challenges—the game.

Tennis is a wonderful sport enjoyed by a lot of wonderful people. You get to meet and become friends with people of all ages and backgrounds. You can travel all over the world and find a game and find people willing to help you. You can play it for the social benefits or play it competitively for the thrill of winning. It takes a lot of time, training and effort to get really good but in my experience it has been worth every minute, every sore muscle and all the time I have put into it, and I hope to play it another thirty years.

Tennis offers some very large financial opportunities for those who have the skills, time, desire and self sacrifice to become very good. It offers so much more to those players who love the sport for what it provides to us all— the opportunity to play the game. But, tell Jerry I'm coming for him!

3 WHAT IS SO WONDERFUL ABOUT
THE GAME OF TENNIS

What's not to love about tennis!

Tennis is truly an international sport that is not only played (at a high level) in the industrialized countries but also in the third world and impoverished countries. It offers interracial, inter-gender, and intergenerational competition and companionship. It provides opportunities to play a sport with people from all walks of life and with all types of experiences. We get to play with company presidents and janitors' young kids and old veterans of tennis as well as up and coming tennis stars. We are all just tennis players on the court.

Tennis can be played on inexpensive hard courts, clay courts, grass courts, asphalt courts and even just plain old dirt courts. All you really need is a cheap racquet, a tennis ball, a center net and a court (every city in America has at least one court). What you need more than anything else is a desire to play.

Tennis offers a path to riches for men, women, boys and girls of all ages. Tennis is a sport you can play with just one arm or even in a wheel chair. It is a sport you can play from age 4 till you can't pick up the racquet any longer. --- What's not to love about Tennis!

Encourage your children to play tennis for all the reasons I have described above. It is a great game and a wonderful way to meet people, get exercise and develop a disciplined mind.

I am 68 years old and have been playing tennis for 40 years. I play 4-5 times per week year around. Well, I do drop down to 3-4 times per week during the winter. I love every minute I am on the court. I love the competition (my current NTRP rating is 5.5). I love the camaraderie within the group I play with. There is a consistent and immediate bond when I meet other tennis players in my business life. I love meeting new people when I play in different leagues. Tennis keeps me in shape and provides an outlet from my real life problems. When I am on the tennis court, I forget about everything else and concentrate on my game.

I started playing when I was 28 (1975) in Phoenix, Arizona. My wife had told me to give up golf or her (I was playing every day – 9 holes after work and 36 holes on Saturday and Sunday).

After a month of just sitting around the house, I was going crazy watching television. Then, after watching a tennis match between Ilie Nastase (the original "Bad Boy" of tennis) and Jimmy Connors, I asked myself "how hard can that be"? So I drove down to the local Kmart and bought a T2000 (Jimmy Connors) tennis racquet and a can of 3 tennis balls. We were living in a mobile home park at that time that had a cement tennis court, I would spend 1

– 2 hours each day hitting 3 balls from one side to the other. I would hit them over the net and then walk to the other side and hit them back. I didn't really know what I was doing, but there was something really satisfying about hitting the balls, especially when they went into the other court. Maybe it was because I am Irish and I had a club in my hand, or maybe it was the challenge of simply getting the ball over the net and into the other court.

About a month later, I was back at Kmart in the sporting goods area and happened to see a bag of loose tennis balls. A light went off and I realized I could use more than 3 tennis balls at a time to practice with. All this time, I had been hitting 3 balls, walking to the other side, and hitting them back. Now, all of a sudden, I realized I could hit a lot more balls in the same time frame – wow what a thought! Little epiphanies became a trend in my tennis career.

I had originally talked my wife into letting me take up tennis because it seemed so cheap. After all, all I needed was 3 balls and 1 racquet. After 30 plus racquets, thousands of balls, clothes, trips, tournaments fees, untold string jobs, tape resin, bags, tape, winter court fees and tin upon tin of Tiger Balm—and shoes, did I forget to mention shoes—I still tell my wife it's cheap compared to our National Debt.

My wife puts up with this obsession because she knows how much I love the game. My only regret with tennis is that I did not start it earlier in life.

When I was in high school, tennis was for girls, real men did not play tennis. Real men played football, basketball, baseball, ran track or wrestled. Surprisingly enough, it is thought of the same way today. Neither one of my sons wanted to take it up for the same reasons. It wasn't until I got past the beginning level of the game and tried to get better that I realized just how accomplished an athlete you have to be to be good at this game.

I read a guest article in *Tennis Magazine* last year about a high school football senior in Illinois. During his junior year, he had already received a football scholarship to a Division I school. However, the summer after his junior year, he incurred an injury that ended his football career. Not to be held down, this amazing athlete switched to basketball. By the end of his senior year, he had received a Division I basketball scholarship. This kid was an obvious athlete with great talent. However, the story was not so much about this kid, but about how this situation could never happen in tennis. No matter how good an athlete you are, there is just too much to learn and too much to master in tennis for it to be possible to become a Division I scholarship player in such a short time. The article went on to describe all the effort, skills and athleticism required to become a good tennis player. But his summary line said it best "Tennis, play if you can".

As I said earlier, I am 68 years old. Even after playing competitive tennis for 40years, I still have more shots to conquer. I always wish I would have started playing earlier. So, after 40 years, what's not to love about tennis!

I think I made the right choice – she's still here.

4 GETTING STARTED

My introduction to tennis was created by a desire to get off the couch and do something inexpensive. It doesn't matter that my initial thought about tennis (being inexpensive) was faulty, because from the first ball I hit, my love of the game has continued to grow. Through many trials and frustrations since I hit that first ball, my love of tennis and the desire to improve is still growing to this day.

To get you started, the one thing all new tennis players should do, and it's free, is to watch the professionals on television. Doing that was a great help to me when I started.

When I started, the VCR was not available to the public, let alone TiVo. I had to watch real time or miss out. I would watch and study the pros movements, strokes, hand position, the arching of their back when they served and how they would bend their knees when hitting a forehand and backhand. Generally, I would watch their form, noting how smooth they were during a stroke because they were not jerky like me. I would get up in the middle of the living room and pretend I was in a game and mimic the movement of the pro I was watching.

Down on the court, I'd picture in my mind the movement and form I had seen and try to get my body to duplicate that form, regardless of where the ball went. To this day, when I take my warm up serves, I concentrate more on my form than getting the ball into the service court, because I know if my form is correct the ball will go where it is supposed to.

This is kind of like shadow boxing. The mind can envision the movement and see the pro's actions and form converting those images into controlling the body's movement and thus the form. In doing this, you will begin to feel the right stroke or proper serve form before you start getting the ball to go where you want. Your body will begin to resolve the inconsistencies between your form and the pros movements and make the compromises that are best for your body. Don't be disappointed that your form is not exactly like the pro's. Your body will make adaptations to fit your it's capabilities and you will end up with a stroke that is mechanically sound for you. Again, to this day, when I start to make mistakes on my strokes or my serve, I take a deep breath and start to concentrate on my form until the smoothness of the stroke returns.

After you have gone through this mind control tennis, then you can start listening to your club pro as to how to tweak your shots, because now your body will have the ability to incorporate minor tweaks in your mechanics to improve your game. Remember to listen to your body, it will tell you when you are doing the right movement to improve your stroke.

5 COURT ETIQUETTE

To further your game, one of the first things you should be doing is finding other players to hit with. First, because that is a great way to improve your game and second, because it is a lot cheaper than taking an excessive amount of lessons just to get in your hitting time.

As a beginning tennis player, one of the surest ways to alienate other tennis players is to display bad tennis manners/etiquette. Poor court etiquette will upset experienced players and makes it harder to gain the support of players you are going to need help from. Below I have address key behaviors "manners/etiquette" that every tennis player should be aware of and follow – in no apparent order:

First, Tennis is a game of honor!

In tennis we "call our own lines", which means that we make decisions affecting the game and our opponent by deciding if a ball is "in" or "out". The general rule in tennis is that if you do not see the ball clearly "out" then it is "in", even if your view was obstructed, if you did not see it clearly go "out" then it is "in".

Tennis is based on the honesty of each player and the quickest way to lose playing and practice partners is to be known as a cheater. Understand that we all make mistakes in calls because the ball is moving pretty fast and some calls are very close to the line. Do not let the desire to win overshadow your judgment to be honest.

- When playing next to other players, do not venture onto the adjacent court to retrieve an errant ball without first asking (or getting an ok nod) permission to do so.

- When an errant ball lands in your court, do not automatically throw or hit the ball back onto the court from which it came. If they are still playing their point, put the ball in your pocket, or throw it to the back of your court, or roll the ball to the back of their court (as long as you do not distract them from playing their point) so that you can continue your game. After your point is finished or when the other court is ready, then you can throw or hit the ball back to the other court.

- Do not ask players on other courts to stop their play to retrieve your ball or racquet. You may warn players on another court if your ball may be in a dangerous position on their court and there is a possibility of them stepping on it and injuring themselves. You can quickly do this by yelling "heads up".

- Stay off an adjacent court if at all possible (sometimes getting to a ball during a point pulls you into another court), if you do go onto another court during a point, be sure to apologize for the interruption after your point.

- When exiting the playing area, avoid walking across someone else's court. If you must cross another court, be sure to wait until given permission to cross and then jog or walk quickly to minimize the interruption to the other players' game.

- When waiting to cross another group's court, do not go to the back of the court and stand against the back wall on the playing court or walk behind players at the back of a court. If you do, you are still in the playing field and are a distraction to the player on the court. Instead, wait by the net until the point is finished or there is a break in the action, then after getting an ok from the players, quickly cross the court to your destination. This is quicker and less of a distraction to the players on the court. Note: this is a big problem at many clubs and tournaments and for people of all ages. Understand, you do not want to interrupt or distract the other players.

- As competitive and frustrating as tennis can be, we all must try and control our emotions. Swearing loudly is frowned upon especially in mixed company (whether the people are on your court or just in hearing distance). You really need to understand the sensitivities of your group and any players or spectators in the area. Sometimes it's hard to exercise verbal control, but every effort should be made to use some other form of emotional release.

- Proper shoes should always be used when on a tennis court, especially do not use shoes that leave marks on the court.

- Always supply balls every other time when playing someone repeatedly.

- Throwing your racquet at another player is not allowed and neither is throwing your racquet onto another court. In general, throwing your racquet is not advised and is considered a delay in the game and bad manners.

However, hitting your racquet hard on the ground to relieve some emotions/tensions is acceptable albeit expensive and annoying.

- It is considered impolite and inconsiderate to cheer when a player makes a mistake or loses a point on an unforced error. You can, however, cheer for the player who is forcing the other player to make a mistake because of their great shot making – but know the difference.

- Do not make noise when players are serving (unless you are lucky enough to be at a Davis Cup match, but still quiet down during the serve).

- As a player, always do your best not to distract a player during a point. Distracting a player can result in a point being awarded to your opponent

- Immediately and clearly call a ball either "out" or "in" – do not take time to make up your mind. By rule, if you don't see the ball go "out", then it is "in"!!!

- Use courtesy and assume the honest intent of all. (Personal note: all of us make mistakes and miscalls, but if I think the person I am playing is intentionally cheating, I will finish the match and will not play that person again. If you are facing a dishonest person in a tournament, request an umpire from the tournament director.).

- Keep the courts clean, pick up your old balls and used tennis cans.

- Remember to use good sportsmanship at all times.

- Always shake the hand of your opponent or, like so many players do today, just a simple fist bump is a sign of respect for the other player.

6 HOW MUCH MONEY AND TIME IS THIS GOING TO COST

One of the real issues that has kept people out of tennis for the longest time, has been that it is thought of as a country club sport. It has been marketed and sold that way for as long as I can remember, mostly because in the distant past it was only played at country clubs. And the high cost of joining a country club just for tennis has kept a lot of people out of the sport.

Over the last fifty years, there has been an enormous effort to build tennis courts in every city and town in this nation. There are thousands of tennis tournaments, clinics and lessons given every day at parks and recreation areas throughout the country, all aimed at getting more people involved with the sport. The Williams sisters (Venus and Serena) began on public courts and look what they have accomplished.

That said, the cost of a tennis racquet ranges from $30.00 to $300.00 and you will need more than one. Indoor court time typically ranges from $20.00 to $36.00

an hour in areas outside of big cities. However, if you are in a city like New York, Chicago or Atlanta court times at the upscale clubs can go to the $200 per hour range; and you will need more than one hour a week. Note: costs in all big city's upscale clubs are quite a bit higher than the rest of the tennis country. Teaching lessons range from $15.00 per hour for group lessons to $120.00 per hour for private lessons. Shoes can run you $40 to more than $150 per pair and, if you play a lot on hard courts, you can easily go through six pairs a year. Amateur tournament entry fees typically range from $20 to $60, not counting time and gas to get to and from the tournament. Lodging expenses will vary according to your needs. We haven't even talked about the clothes, balls, grips and stringing costs. Tennis can become pretty expensive – if you let it.

TT I now play with a $70 racquet (I have four). I didn't always play with such a cheap racquet but based on my criteria for a racquet this one has worked out the best for me (see the chapter on "Choosing the Right Tennis Racquet). So, you don't have to have the most expensive racquet to play your best. Realize most tennis players will go through several racquet types throughout their tennis life.

TT Play outdoors as much as possible where the court time is usually free or very inexpensive. A lot of the community centers now have courts that are well kept and mostly free or for a small fee. During the winter months, if you have to play indoors, sign up for a league sub at a tennis club for their permanent court groups (most of the time subs do not have to pay). You will be essentially on call and won't be able to plan your time as well but you also will not have to spend as much money on court time.

Shoes are vital to the health of the player. You can easily spend two to four hours sprinting, stopping, pivoting and jumping each time you get on a court. Don't skimp on the price of the shoes if they are the right fit. However, you do not need to buy name brand shoes to get the right fit. I have found buying online at www.tenniswarehouse.com or www.Holabirdsports.com can save a lot of money. Just make sure that you identify the right shoe first at Dicks, Foot Locker or some other local sporting shoe store before you buy online.

As for lesson costs, spend as much time as possible in group lessons. Once you decide on a teaching pro you like, let them know how much you have to spend and maybe you can cut a deal by feeding balls to younger players or working tournaments for lesson time or just helping out.

Tournament costs will be based simply on how many tournaments you want or need to play and at what level. The major tournaments cost more and are generally in the bigger cities, so travel expenses are higher. Parents, you can do a lot of car pooling and sharing travel costs.

These tips alone can save you hundreds of dollars a year.

Thus, tennis is not cheap, but it also does not have to cost a fortune. Watch where and what you spend your money on, and you can enjoy the game of tennis on a fairly light sports budget.

7 CHOOSING THE RIGHT TENNIS RACQUET

As long as we are talking about changing things, let's talk about your choice of racquets. First of all, I always carry at least three racquets. Two strung at one tension, high (tight) for control and the third strung looser for more power. I do this because during tournaments when I play people who strike the ball very hard, I need a little extra control and when I play some people that play a strictly defensive game, I need to generate more power. Plus, I always need an extra racquet in case I break a string (which is quite often). This way my style (aggressive) of play and strokes can remain the same and the depth of the shot will remain constant.

Just as a side comment, a newly open can of balls will become less responsive the longer you play with them. Consequently, if you are playing a hard hitter, in the third set the balls will not return off your racquet the same as in the first set. That's when I change to a racquet with different tension to give me more power in the third and deciding set.

Before purchasing the racquet your club pro is suggesting, understand that they may be making money when selling you a racquet, plus most of the club pros have racquet deals with manufacturers and only represent and sell specific brands (be aware that they may and I emphasize "may" have a vested interest in suggesting a certain type of racquet and it is not you they are vested in). However, most teaching pros have developed a sound knowledge base of racquet choices over their time teaching and playing, so do talk to them about your racquet choices.

TT Try to find someone knowledgeable and experienced in tennis who doesn't make any money when suggesting a particular racquet. You will find that most of the good players in your club or area will be more than happy to offer advice on equipment. Mostly because they had to learn it the hard way, by buying equipment that didn't work for them. Just ask them to spend five minutes with you, you won't regret the time. The most expensive, latest technology racquet will more than likely not make you play better. Thus choosing the most expensive upfront is probably not the wisest idea. Also, understand, it is not uncommon to change racquets as your skill improves.

I have also found the internet to be a great source of information on tennis racquets. There are some good sites to try first. I like www.Tenniswarehouse.com, www.Holabirdsports.com and www.Tennisexpress.com which can offer some good prices and information. These are good sites because they offer great prices and user reviews. Tennis Warehouse also has a demo program (for the cost of postage) that lets you try almost any racquet they sell. This way you can try out a lot of racquets for just the postage costs. The more racquets you demo at one time, the better the deal. Believe me you need to find the right racquet for your game.

I believe that the most important aspects of a racquet are its weight, swing-weight, head size and grip size. Begin by going down to your local sports store (Dick's, Dunham's, etc.) and simply swing several different racquets, taking note of the grip size (printed on the inside of the racquet's throat), brand and model of the ones you like. Note: don't worry about the string pattern or the NTRP rating level; just find the racquet you like to swing. Then go to one of the web sites I mentioned earlier and search for those racquets to get more information about them.

When you find them (you can even go onto EBay or Amazon and find used ones), click on the picture of the racquet and locate the weight, swing-weight, length, head size, stiffness and whether it is head heavy (HH) or head light (HL). **Note: the direction of measurement for a tennis racquet is from the head to the handle.** Head heavy and head light is measured in points (pts). A point is 1/8", so a 4 point HL racquet is balanced ½" below the center point of the racquet (towards the head), thus it is head light. And 2 points head heavy means that the racquet is balanced ¼" above the center point (towards the handle). Also, pay attention to the proper grip size of the racquet. Too small and you will get too much wrist action and too big you won't be able to get enough wrist action. I have found that for my game, I need a little more wrist action, so I err on the small side.

Now you have the key parameters to search the web and other manufacturers for similar racquets to the one you liked at the sports store. At the www.tenniswarehouse.com site, you can go to the "Racquet Finder" button on the Home page and enter the parameters you recorded from your trip to your local sports store. The computer will find similar racquets for you to try out. Demo these racquets and determine the one you like best. Another site to try is www.tennis.com/yourgame/gear/racquetfinder/.

TT TWEAKERS - (Tweakers are people who have been playing the game for quite a while and have mostly settled in on their game and equipment, but continue to want to improve in small steps.) For us Tweakers, we can start to change the string types, string composition and combinations of strings that we feel will help fine tune our game - there are a lot of choices in strings.

There is even an equation that allows Tweakers to select a racquet that provides more comfort for our elbows and more power for our serves. Read about this equation at www.racquetresearch.com/complete_idiot.htm. It is a well written paper and deserves some time for Tweakers. There are a lot of different string variations (type, material, design, weight and tension) you can experiment with. As I stated earlier, I use one tension (60lbs) for power players and a lower tension (58lbs) for defensive players that hit a relatively soft shot. That two pound difference can significantly change the flight and distance of the ball.

The "Head Light" (HL) and "Head Heavy" (HH) balance question is something we need to understand. As discussed in the article at www.racquetresearch.com, the choice of HL or HH needs to be considered in light of your physical capabilities and desired style of game. Such as, are you a "baseline" player or a "serve & volley" player? Do you consider yourself an "all court" player or a "defensive" player?

Do you hit with a lot of "top spin" (lots of wrist action) or with a "flat" stroke (little wrist action)? Understanding of your game will help you determine the characteristics you need in a racquet to help your game.

By arranging the different combinations of these characteristics (weight, swing-weight, length, head size, stiffness, HH, HL) with your style of game and physical abilities, you can maximize your performance on the court with the right choice of a racquet. As my game evolved from a serve and volley to a baseline game, my racquet changed from a 26 inch, 11.2 oz, 2-points HH with a 95 square inch head size to a 27.0 inch, 10.3 oz, 1-point HL racquet with a 108 square inch head size and swing-weight of 318.

For my game is still an aggressive style with a flat stroke. I use the heaviest racquet I can swing that will give me the most top spin (choice of strings and a little head light) and racquet control during three hours of tennis. Realize, all of us want to stroke the ball the same way in the third hour as we did in the first hour.

Once you have familiarized yourself with the complexities and importance of selecting a racquet, you can then have another discussion with your club pro about the racquets they offer and why. Since your racquet is generally the most expensive piece of equipment you will buy, you should spend a fair amount of time finding the right one. Don't be afraid to try new racquets. Keep in mind you have to like your racquet if you want to play well.

8 FINDING A GOOD TEACHING PROFESSIONAL

There are a lot of touring professionals, college players, and teenage tennis assistants teaching tennis today. There are certified USPTA teaching professionals, there are old battle worn players teaching tennis and there are men and women who have been teaching tennis for the last 15 to 20 years wherever they could find a court.

There are clubs, resorts, schools and academies where you can go to learn tennis and improve your game. Try http://usptafindapro.com/index.cfm/MenuItemID/654/MenuGroup/Find-a-Pro.htm to find a professional recommended by the USPTA.

There are the tennis professionals who like to teach with a single belief system forcing their students to become their worshipers. These professionals have big egos and spend most of their time talking about their system and very little time worried about your system. There are the professionals who, like army drill instructors work the students until they drop.

There are the professionals who just feed balls at the student relentlessly without offering any instruction on form and how to hit different shots. There are the professionals who generally have entrenched themselves into a club and work for the money over everything else and there are professionals that will show a genuine interest in your child and try to help them with the specifics they need to get to the next level.

All of these "teaching pros" come at different prices with different motivations, so, as you can see, choosing a teaching professional can be very difficult and confusing. Finding a "good" teaching professional is like finding a good racquet. What's right for one person may not be right for another.

When selecting a professional for your child, the age of your child will make a difference in the choice of the professional. Some professionals are good with pre-adolescent children and others do best with adolescents while others are better with adults than children. Ask around, most players will let you know their opinion of the different local professionals.

First of all don't be afraid to try out different professionals. Most professionals will not want you to bounce around because it may diminish what they are trying to teach you, plus you are spending your money somewhere else. But realize, you must find a "teaching professional" that is right for you and or your child's level.

I would suggest you start by going to local tournaments and finding the tournament director. Ask any of the players who the director is and they will point you in the right direction. It is usually someone that has been very involved with the local tennis community for some time.

Ask them for advice about the local teaching professionals. Try to ask questions that revolve around your skill level and where you want to grow. A lot of teaching professionals specialize in a particular age group or fit into one of the categories mentioned above (Lots of drills, feeders, system instructors or just hitters). You should have a concept in your mind as to what you are trying to learn or improve on. That is, are you looking for someone to help with your general mechanics or your serve, learn a new backhand or just get started? Different instructors are better at teaching different aspects of the game, so know what you are trying to accomplish before you start looking for an instructor.

If you can't find a local tournament director, then go down to the local parks and look for some decent tennis players over the age of forty (40). Most good players over forty have been playing the game a while because they love it. They are typically more than willing to offer their opinion of who the good instructors are in the area. Ask a few people to get a general feel for who most of the good players like. The people that love the sport know that the future of the sport is getting in new blood at any age. The older players generally do not have a financial stake in their answers, just a love for the sport.

There are a lot of good teaching professionals at your local tennis clubs, but remember they have a financial stake in selling you. I recommend signing up for a series of group lessons, 1) because it is less expensive, 2) because group lessons are generally taught by multiple professionals so you will have chance to see each of their teaching styles and 3) because you will be with other players and have the opportunity to talk about the tennis community.

Realize the best decision is an informed decision.

9 THE ROLE OF EMOTIONAL OUTBURSTS

Personally, I like to see emotion expressed on the court. However, watching your child go off half cocked can be disconcerting and embarrassing for you and disrespectful to other players—and it should be, if your child is out of control. However, controlled outbursts, when understood can be good for your child. Controlled outbursts can act as a focal point for the mind and release tension, thus when properly utilized an emotional outburst can get the mind and body working together.

Competitive tennis is a very personal sport. It's you against the other person where every shot counts not to mention that there may also be a number of people watching you play. It is a time when the biggest adversary on the court is not your opponent—it is you.

Consider this; the competitive tennis player is constantly working toward playing a better game. To do that, there are the basic strokes (forehand, backhand, overhead, volley, half volley) to master. Then, there are the variations in the strokes (topspin, flat, slice, moon, twist). There is also the pace of the ball--should you hit it hard, take something off the stroke or try to drive it through your opponent. Next, there is keeping your balance and positioning while moving forward, backward and side to side when you strike the ball. All the while keeping in mind where your opponent is on the court. Eventually you have to hit the ball to someplace that will give you the best chance to win the point. Right after you hit the ball, you have to go on defense and get to the right spot on the court to give you the best opportunity to return your opponents shot. Then there is the next shot!

Obviously tennis is a very complex game requiring a lot of different skills. That is why it is so frustrating and so much fun at the same time. Getting all the complexities of a shot correct every time is almost impossible, but the drive to do it right is very strong in competitive personalities. Repeated mistakes can result in a high level of frustration, especially when self corrections are not working. This when an emotional outburst is most common. As long as the actions following an outburst are directed to improve one's self or relieve tension, then we need not worry. We need to recognize that the emotional outburst is rooted in passion and a desire to do things correctly, which is a sign of a competitive personality. The actions you, as a parent, should see are a refocusing on the game, a new calmness, a decrease in small outbursts or even a smile.

The new player and parent needs to understand that everybody make mistakes, even Federer, Nadal, the Williams sisters (Venus and Serena) and Maria Sharapova. All players at all levels double fault, swing and miss overheads, hit the ball deep or into the net. The younger and more inexperienced player will almost certainly want and/or need to release the frustration from within when these things happen. However, the key is to get them to train their mind to release the frustration and refocus the effort. If done right, the body calms down and the mind refocuses and the strokes begin to work again.

If left unguided and untrained, emotional outbursts can be redirected internally and continue to increase in frequency and intensity. They will result in a negative self-image which will manifest itself in a loss of trust in one's self, a loss of focus and thus a very erratic and inconsistent game.

Consequently, as a parent, you need to understand what type of emotional outburst your child is expressing. Parents need to use these situations to improve the child's perspective on the game and explain the amount of hard work it takes to be successful in tennis and life.

Players need to recognize how emotion plays into their game and if it is beneficial or detrimental. If they are out of control, then they need to make changes to get back into control and use emotion to positively influence their game. Without emotion, there is nothing to drive a player through the long hours and hard work required to improve and develop the ability to last out a full match.

Emotion can be a great motivator and needs to be present in one's game. The level of emotion can be discussed and modified for each personality, but, again, I believe it should be there. How we channel these outbursts is what helps us win or spins us into an emotional hole of mistakes and self-degradation. Tennis is a fantastic game where passion, desire and anger play a large role. Learning to use emotion to improve your game can turn that emotional outburst to be elation at winning.

10 HOW TO STAY FOCUSED

Remember the acronym PGSMT (Point, Game, Set, Match, and Tournament). If you take care of the point, the point will take care of the game; the game will take care of the set, the set will take care of the match; and the match will take care of the tournament. Meaning, don't worry about winning the tournament, focus on winning the point.

I was talking with the mother of a young lady (fourteen years old) whom I coached a little when she was nine. We were at a local tournament where the young lady was playing.

The mother and I were talking about how easy it is to lose your focus during a game, let alone a match or a complete tournament. We were talking about why the real easy, no brainer shots are missed when, sure enough, her daughter missed an easy, high floating volley at the net (she volleyed it long). We both cringed, but the daughter just smiled and continued. Her mother and I continued to talk about how she could help her daughter get through these little brain lapses. We talked about what runs through a players mind when that easy shot presents itself.

It would be nice if the only thing in a player's mind at that time was simply "hit the ball". Unfortunately, what occurs is a series of thoughts such as should I hit it hard, should I hit it deep or drop it just over the net, should I punch it or take a full swing, should I use a backhand or a forehand, where is the other player, and is my mother watching. All of these thoughts occur within milliseconds. Consequently, the probability of sorting through all those choices within the time required will not happen and you will more often than not hit the ball into the net or drive it long. Then you will start kicking yourself, calling yourself all kinds of names and even contemplating quitting the game, all because you missed an easy, no brainer shot. The smart player will just smile and move onto the next point. I would like to say this is age dependent but that would not be true. This happens at all ages and with both genders. It is a problem of focus.

The secret to not missing these easy shots is to train the mind to first, recognize an easy shot, second, calm down because easy shots are easy to miss, third, watch the ball (consciously tell yourself to focus on the ball), fourth, concentrate on the ball, fifth, focus on the ball and sixth, "hit the ball". Don't get cute, don't try a touch shot, do not try a patty-cake drop shot, just take a crisp volley and "hit the ball". Actually, steps one, two and three are the critical ones and have to happen very quickly. Once the recognition and calmness sets in the rest will follow as your training kicks in.

During a match, we all have let downs when we are behind and frustrated or ahead and thinking about our next opponent, or thinking about something outside of tennis. Whatever the reason, we start to lose focus on the task at hand, hitting the ball correctly and winning the point. If you play without focus, you will lose the point, game and match. It is vital to regain your focus, or better yet, not lose it. That is why I think Tiger Woods is such a great golfer. His ability to focus and stay focused throughout an entire tournament is absolutely what sets him apart from everyone else. It is not his strokes, it's his ability to focus.

For tennis players the strokes make a big difference, the ability to hit the ball correctly will offer huge advantages, but the ability to focus will win the important matches.

The first thing you must do to improve your focus is to recognize when you are losing focus. You must train your mind to recognize when you are thinking of something other than winning the point at hand. You must learn to recognize that if you are having trouble deciding whether to hit the ball down the center or out wide, into the body, use a spin serve or flat or high bounce, you are losing focus.

If you are struggling with deciding what type of return of serve to do—cross court, down the line, to the center, lob, top spin, slice, short, deep or hard, you are losing focus.

If, during the game, you are thinking about class work, homework, your teacher, your friends, work or something other than the point, then you are losing your focus.

If you are not thinking about your next stroke or where you should be on the court, your mind is drifting and you are losing your focus.

The fundamentals of the game are always about adjusting. Rarely does a ball come at you when you are in the perfect position with the right grip, balanced correctly and ready to hit the ball. In tennis, you are always on the move. There is always some adjustment you have to make. Move left or right, run forward, backup, twist the body, dig low, jump high, switch from forehand to backhand, etc. It is endless and consistent. When we drill, we practice hitting each shot completely set up for the shot, but in a match the ball is seldom where we want it to be. So, why would we think staying focused is any easier?

What can you do about losing focus?

As I said earlier, you must train your mind to recognize these situations as a loss of focus. Then you can take action to re-establish your focus. When I start to lose focus, which seems to happen more often as I get older, I start a silent chant. I say to myself over and over "Senor Avanti", "Senor Avanti", "Senor Avanti". This phrase is an eighteenth century prayer Spanish monks used to help them pray continually with every step as they walked through their day. It was their way of keeping God in their thoughts at all times. The point of the chant for me is that it is easy to remember, easy to say and easy to repeat, which then re-focuses my mind by eliminating all those other distracting thoughts. Now for you, you need to find some method that you can use to re-focus your mind after you recognize that you are losing focus.

Some people use a chant like I do, some people pinch themselves, and some hit themselves on the head with their racquet strings, some slap their knees, some take a long pause between points to regain their composure, and some switch to another racquet to force their minds to make a change. It doesn't matter what it is, you simply need to determine what you can consciously do to refocus your mind.

Realize, there is a difference between losing focus and losing a point. If you are losing multiple points, you might want to change your racquet or change your grip or even your toss on the serve, but when you are losing your focus, you need to change your state of mind.

I told the mother to watch her daughter's body language for signs of anger or depression that last more than a couple of points. If the daughter continued to think about the missed no brainer shot, it would start to affect the rest of her game. Fortunately, the daughter just smiled and went on with the next point. She had not lost her focus just the point and she went on to win the tournament.

11 HISTORY OF TENNIS

The term "tennis" derives from the French word tenez, which means "take heed", a warning from the server to the receiver.

References to the game can be found as early as the reign of King Alexander III (1249-86) whose mother Marie of Couci may well have introduced the game to Scotland from France.

From the different theories for the beginning of tennis, the most probable is that tennis was derived from a form of handball in 13th century France. The game came into being in the monastery courtyards of France. The monks usually stretched a rope across the cloistered central quadrangles in the monastery or sometimes played immediately adjacent to a castle. This monastic pastime known as "real" or "royal" tennis, was adopted enthusiastically by royalty and their court, who dubbed the new sport, jeu de paume, meaning "the game of the palm." It was played indoors in long narrow rooms.

During the 13th century, the popularity of tennis spread at a fever pitch to a point where both monarchs and authorities of the Church felt compelled to ban tennis among their subjects. It had become so popular in the French monasteries that more than one cleric was known to have shirked his monastic duties in favor of playing. As a result, the Archbishop of Rouen in 1245 prohibited his priests from engaging in this diversion. For much the same reason, King Louis IX outlawed the sport. Two kings lost their lives as a result of tennis, King Louis X of France (1314-16) and Charles VIII of France (1483-98). It is said that Louis X died of a chill immediately after playing an energetic game of jeu de paume at Château de Vincennes. Charles VIII died after striking his head on a horizontal piece of wood over the door which led to his tennis court.

By the 14th century, tennis had found its way to England where both Henry VII and Henry VIII apparently became keen players and instigated the building of courts up and down the country. Supposedly, Henry VIII himself invented the 'service'. His servants used to throw the ball up in the air for him because he was too fat to do it himself.

The game was outlawed in England in 1388 because the people were failing to practice archery, an invaluable skill in warfare. In Paris, citizens were hit with a similar ordinance in 1397, because they were neglecting their families and jobs.

These and succeeding edicts were virtually ignored, and tennis continued to flourish. Walled-in courts began to appear in France in 1368, and by 1600 there were two thousand indoor and outdoor courts throughout the country. Never losing sight of its royal appeal, the tennis ball itself was standardized by King Louis XI (1461-1483) of France. Balls were made of soft cloth sewn into a hard round shape. As to the construction of tennis courts, the Valois Kings François I (1515-1547) and Henry II (1547-1559) sought to outshine all their princely rivals, commissioning the celebrated French architect Jacques Androuet du Cerceau to design beautiful courts in the gardens of many French châteaux. Henry II was seen as one of the best paume-players of his age. He liked to play before as many people as possible.

Royal interest in England began with Henry V (1413-22), but it was Henry VIII (1509-47) who made the biggest impact as a young monarch. He played the game with gusto at Hampton Court on a court he had built in 1530, and on several other courts in his palaces. It is believed that his second wife Anne Boleyn was watching a game of real tennis when she was arrested and that Henry was playing tennis when news was brought to him of her execution. During the reign of James I (1603-25), there were 14 courts in London.

In France, François I (1515-47) was an enthusiastic player and promoter of real tennis, building courts and encouraging play among the courtiers and commoners. His successor, Henry II (1547-59), was also an excellent player and continued the royal French tradition. During his reign, the first known book about tennis, Trattato del Giuoco della Palla was written in 1555 by an Italian priest, Antonio Scaino da Salo.

King Charles IX granted a constitution to the Corporation of Tennis Professionals in 1571, creating the first pro tennis 'tour' and establishing three levels of professionals, apprentice, associate, and master. The first codification of the rules of real tennis was written by a professional named Forbet and published in 1599.

Real tennis courts (jeu à dedans) are very substantial buildings (a larger area than a lawn tennis court, with walls and a ceiling to contain all but the highest lob shots). They are enclosed by walls on all sides, three of which have sloping roofs (known as "penthouses") with various openings, and a buttress (tambour) off which shots may be played. The courts (except at Falkland Palace, a jeu quarré design) share the same basic layout but have slightly different dimensions. The courts are about 110 by 39 feet (33.5 × 11.9 m) including the penthouses, or about 96 by 32 feet (29.3 × 9.8 m) on the playing floor, varying by a foot or two per court. They are doubly asymmetric—not only is one end of the court different in the shape from the other, but the left and right sides of the court are also different.

In Victorian England (1837 – 1901), public interest shifted to the outdoor game of lawn tennis which quickly became the most popular form of the sport.

Tennis as the modern sport can be dated to two separate roots. Between 1859 and 1865, Major Harry Gem and his friend, Augurio Perera, developed a game that combined elements of rackets similar to the game of Poona or Badminton many British soldiers brought from having been stationed in India and the Basque ball game pelota, which they played on Perera's croquet lawn in Birmingham, United Kingdom. In 1872, along with two local doctors, they founded the world's first tennis club in Leamington Spa.

For the amusement of his guests at a garden party on his estate of Nantclwyd, in Llanelidan, Wales, in December 1873, Major Walter Clopton Wingfield designed a similar game — which he called sphairistike (Greek: σφάιριστική, meaning "skill at playing at ball") and was soon known simply as "sticky".

He was probably the first person to write down a set of rules for lawn tennis—one of which stated that only the server could score a point. The main difference from Real Tennis was that the court didn't have side or end walls. But, as a marked difference to the modern game, the shape of the court was an "hourglass", the length being 20 yards but the width being 30 yards at the end and only 21 yards at the net.

In 1875 Henry Jones asked the community to accept the new sport of (lawn) tennis. Two years later the Croquet Club became the Croquet and Tennis Club.

In 1877, the first tournament was held at Wimbledon to raise money for the pony roller. A pony roller is used to keep the courts in good condition. During this tournament, there were problems with the fact that there were many different types of rules being used in tennis. Rules weren't the only thing that was being debated. The other thing they had to decide was where the service line should be placed, how high the net should be and if they should have one or two serves to get into the service box. Scoring was another issue. When making the court, they still debated whether or not to make it rectangular or an hourglass. During this time, these rules abandoned the hourglass court shape standardizing it at 78 x 27 feet and have remained unchanged in any significant fashion with the exception of the tie break introduced in the 1970s (except for the Davis Cup - 1989).

In 1874, a US traveler brought the game to the Americas and the US Lawn Tennis Association was formed in 1881. International competition soon followed, with the International Lawn Tennis Challenge Trophy (later the Davis Cup) first contested in 1900 and the Wightman Cup, for competition between British and American women's teams, in 1923. Men's singles and doubles play was included on the program for the first modern Olympic Games in 1896.

Go to http://www.tennistheme.com/tennishistory.html. for additional information about the history of tennis.

12 HISTORY OF SCORING

All varieties of medieval tennis used "chases". This is a complicated and unusual system of scoring in which, if the ball is not returned on the volley or after the first bounce, a chase is marked on the ground, either at the point of the second bounce or the point at which the ball stops rolling. The chase itself is not a point and the score does not alter until the players change ends and the chase is played off. If the player succeeds in making his own ball bounce or stop nearer the base-line or the back of the court than the chase laid by his opponent, then he wins the point and the score is altered accordingly. This method of "playing chases" is common to all forms of medieval tennis, the chase itself being mentioned as early as 1316.

Scoring in fifteens is also old and is mentioned in a poem about the Battle of Agincourt written in 1415 by Jean Le Maingre. It seems that the scoring in fifteens went 15, 30, 45 but over time, instead of saying "forty-five", people started to say forty" for short and eventually this stuck.

But why fifteens? Well, no one really knows. Some have said that it is based around the clock face, with a quarter move of the hand to indicate a score of fifteen, thirty, and forty-five. When the hand moved to sixty, the game was over. This explanation seems unlikely since medieval France predates the advent of mechanical clocks, with sundials being the chronometer of choice at the time.

Another common explanation is that the scoring system was based on the different gun calibers of the British naval ships. When firing a salute, the ships first fired their 15-pound guns on the main deck, followed by the 30-pound guns of the middle deck, and finally by the 40-pound lower gun deck.

A more plausible hypothesis points to a French origin, since in the early middle ages, 60 was a very key number in France in the same way that 100 is today. That's why the words for seventy, eighty and ninety in French are based on sixty, e.g. seventy is "soixante-dix" or "sixty and ten" so it makes sense that a game might be to sixty points. But then, why divide by four?

The most likely theory has to do with betting, since most sports including tennis were played for money in the Middle Ages. There were laws in nearby Germany in the 14th and late 13th centuries that forbade stakes greater than sixty "deniers", which supports the theory. It so happens that at about the same time, there was a coin in circulation called a "gros denier tournois" which was worth 15 deniers. Perhaps those in the French tennis playing public were playing for one "gros denier tournois" per point up to the maximum stake of sixty deniers for a game.

And what of the sources of the words "love" and "deuce"?

Deuce is derived from the French "a deux du jeu"—two points away from game, or de unx , the English having shortened it first to "a deus" ("deus" being deux in old French) and then, thoroughly incorrectly, to "deuce".

Because of the deuce rule, tennis is one of several sports of which it could be said that a match could theoretically never finish. Another example is baseball, whose rules do not allow for a tied game.

Love similarly is attributed to the French. That "love" comes from the French for egg, "l'oeuf", is doubtful despite the assumed linkage with the cricketing phrase "out for a duck's egg (duck for short)". The most likely explanation is that it comes from the Dutch/Flemish "lof" which means honour. Around the time that the expression came to be used, England received a wealth of immigrants from the Low Countries due to the trauma caused there by incoming Protestantism. Bearing in mind that most games were played for money, if a player scored no points, the phrase "omme lof spelen" would have been applicable—he "played for the honour".

Actually, it comes from the idea of playing for love, rather than money--the implication being that one who scores zero consistently can only be motivated by a true love for the game.

13 KEEPING SCORE

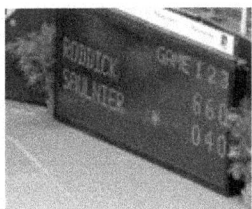

Scoring is identical in the singles and doubles games. A tennis game, when not prolonged by a tie, is played to four points, designated by the terms 15, 30, 40, and game, with zero points being referred to by the term love. A tie at 40 is called deuce. Because a game must be won by two points, play continues from deuce until one player leads by a margin of two points. After reaching deuce, the player who can win the game on the next point is said to have the advantage, while a subsequent tied score is always called deuce. The score of the server is always given first. Typical scores at stages of a given tennis game might be "love-15" or "40-30." The players or teams exchange sides after each odd-numbered game.

Players must win six games to win the set, but they must win by at least two games. Thus, if a set becomes tied at 5-5, at least 7 game victories are required to win the set. A tiebreaker is often employed if a set becomes tied at 6-6. A tiebreaker is generally played to 7 points, but because it too must be won by at least two points, it may be extended. The winner of a tiebreaker is recorded as having won the set 7-6, regardless of the point total achieved in the tiebreaker. Tennis matches are usually the best two out of three sets or the best three out of five sets.

It's still 9 degrees outside, the snow is blowing harder than when I arrived. The roads are snow packed and iffy and I have another forty-five minute drive in front of me. But, I won!

So let it snow. What's not to love about tennis?

ABOUT THE AUTHOR

When I started this book I was 61 years old, I am now 68 which means I have been playing and teaching tennis for 40 years. I currently have a NTRP rating of 5.0. I have had two Achilles operations, one knee operation and a left foot tendon operation. The doctors want to fuse my right wrist and replace my right knee. But, it is snowing outside and I have a long drive to the courts for my next match, so I'll hold off a little longer - what's not to love about tennis!

www.ingramcontent.com/pod-product-compliance
Lightning Source LLC
Chambersburg PA
CBHW071740020426
42331CB00008B/2112